LUCID.

BHAVINI

Copyright © Bhavini
All Rights Reserved.

This book has been published with all efforts taken to make the material error-free after the consent of the author. However, the author and the publisher do not assume and hereby disclaim any liability to any party for any loss, damage, or disruption caused by errors or omissions, whether such errors or omissions result from negligence, accident, or any other cause.

While every effort has been made to avoid any mistake or omission, this publication is being sold on the condition and understanding that neither the author nor the publishers or printers would be liable in any manner to any person by reason of any mistake or omission in this publication or for any action taken or omitted to be taken or advice rendered or accepted on the basis of this work. For any defect in printing or binding the publishers will be liable only to replace the defective copy by another copy of this work then available.

dedicated to the younger, choatic, sensitive girl i was back then - i don't know if i have become more or less of who i was, but i hope i look back and make myself proud. thanks for deciding to drown into writing what you believed were poetry, thank you for not tearing them up as you grew up.

Contents

Contents

Preface

not keeping promises to the self can be good sometimes, i assume, because you have this book in your hand.

it's been almost 5 years since i completed my first raw attempt at publishing, my first taste of the real world. and since then, the manuscript i wrote or the poetry compilation idea i get, i tell myself that i can do it when i am settled and ready, which is not wrong. but in the recent times, i've been trying to work against the perfectionist in me, and this book a good opportunity for me to do that – to do things as i feel is right and not necessarily when they're perfect.

and i sincerely don't expect you accept any of my works to be poetry (imposter syndrome 1, bhavini 0) – have never had a thing for rhyming, nor do i have proper knowledge on what is poetry. poetry in my practical way of working is writing what i feel, in rawness, in sentences that are pretentious, breaking down sentences to give a feel – ultimately, it's about transliterating the feels jumping around my nerves and seeping through my brain.

so there will be hypothetical dialogues, long poetry and short poetry (in my defense, stuff i believe are poetry will be there), and everything else i mustered out of my heartstrings, and yes i can be simultaneously possessing a god complex about my work and self-depriciating image about it too. it's called "multi-tasking".

after this compilation of poetry, i have added 3 things - one is a letter i wrote recently to all things i love; second a poetry which i wrote somewhat recently, a compilcated verse which you may perhaps think as genius or an absolute waste of words, but i added it because i take pride in how i am able to write, which is my evolution and my hope to move forward; a short essay (?) i wrote for a contest (and didn't win obviously) but which i do hold pride in realizing i wrote it; and well, actually, i have added 4 things (but the number feels so incomplete so i said 3) - i have added another short essay i wrote for another contest, something to do with "What has changed for you in the midst of the COVID-19 pandemic, the ongoing racism in the USA, and the recent public response to police violence?"

this *is* a poetry book yes, but i just feel like putting these out too.

so there you go – off to read some little pieces out of my brain, from a very few years/months back in my life.

and in case you haven't figured it out by the end of the book - this book is completely self-absorbing. it's pretty much like a monologue, my own world, where i just put up stuff i feel like and talk about me and for me from the front to the back cover ;)

Acknowledgements

*to the bestest people who kept me sane. special mention to suba varma,
and to mrudhula akka and sowmya akka.*

to the people who love me despite my inability to connect back, i am thankful.

another special mention to shyama, without whose encouragement i wouldn't have been triggered to start again.

Prologue

the girl felt homesick for a place that never existed.

the girl furled her fingers around her pen, and in many cases, typed them down.

vigorously. feverishly.

the girl wrote about things that concerned her, things she would also gaslight herself to tell herself she was being dramatic, needy and vain.

about her body. about her deep sense of sadness. about the romantic love she aspires to have.

the girl has stopped writing. it has been a while.

every time she looks back at what she has written, it hurts her. all she can do is hope to write again and write better.

she forgets to give herself what she deserves to give herself.

she will keep longing, she will keep yearning, she will keep waiting.

she is full of hope. she is full of hope.

1. asking forgiveness - 1

my sister is only six years old and she sits with her legs together –
they teach us that earlier than they teach us anything,
they teach us to be *courteous,* and *proper.*
i bet they didn't teach that to the two-year-old and the eight-year-old,
and everyone falling in every number,
because if they had been taught i wouldn't be reading about them
or watching people think that they care about the world.
my sister is only six years old and she doesn't talk with strangers
she's shy of them and she's cute
karina could've done that – she could've been shy at the boy
and he would've left her without slashing her with a knife
because she turned him down.
my sister is only six years old and she looks at the clouds
i haven't asked her once what shape they are
because every cloud is an eye for me
and everywhere i'm watched.
they didn't teach me to not exist, so i exist
and i'm watched, watched

i cannot tell them to stop giving me that smirk and looking
up and down at my wholesome body
people wouldn't listen
because my name isn't up on the newspapers.
my teacher talks about a creator
tell me – can i go to the creator
and seek forgiveness,
forgiveness that i cannot ask myself,
forgiveness for existing in this nameless piece of flesh
and can i ask for freedom
for being someone who has only meaning when someone
intrudes me
freedom from being someone who can think and love and
dream
freedom from being someone who wants to feel safe,
tell me – can i ask forgiveness
for all sins i did
from someone who i don't believe
someone apparently even more powerful than me
someone?

2. asking myself forgiveness - 2

my teacher talks about a creator
and i don't believe in a creator – i don't have someone to go to
someone who will forgive me for my sins
and i don't have myself to ask forgiveness either.
i have nowhere to go.
i was too young when i rented my house to anxiety
i rented my house because i wanted to protect myself
that is all i wanted – i wanted to feel protected.
i didn't know anxiety will be a permanent resident,
i didn't know it will bring other people to live with.
it's been too long since i had my house now
and i can't breathe inside there.
anxiety and the others have sunk into my skin
and i believe they're me – anxiety and the others
me and my guests have become the same.
we've lived together too long and too close that their stench is
on me
and perhaps my stench is on them.
(and they still love me – that is why they're with me, right?)
i don't have anywhere to go.
i want to go somewhere else
but i think i want to remain there.

i've not had a place to go
or a person to go.
i'm a nomad, nomad.
i have nowhere to go – i have to reclaim my place i know
but i don't, i don't.
i won't.
i don't want the place i'm living in –
it stinks.
and i don't want to live on anyone else.
i want to find a home, a home.

3. you think you're reading happiness but you're reading sadness. you think you're reading sadness but you're reading happiness.

i see people walking with umbrellas under skies as dark as a wet navy blue towel where you can not differentiate the tears from the shower, their smiles shared or unshared with or without knowing that they make a flower bloom beneath a butterfly miles away like they're miles away from themselves, the winds damp and non-existent enough to be subtle and on the brim of being noticed and unnoticed like the leaf atop the tree that first receives the sunlight, their umbrellas shining in the colors of the rain that is colorless before and after touching anything because it shines not because of its contact with matter but in itself like the person who hides the redness in their cheek when they love someone who doesn't love them, their feet detached and feeling different things that their body isn't like the moon and stars that exist in a single sky but while the moon catches love the stars catch dreams and the intersection of love and dreams are lost in the void between them – i see.

4. i'm scared of the demons inside your head, perhaps you see my face in one of those demons.

"lewis capaldi sings, *i was kind of used to being somebody you loved* in my ears when you last called me. you didn't like it when i listened to songs when you were around. you'd play around and get my earphones, and I'd place it on your ears. yesterday you pulled me into your chest and didn't leave me until we were both laughing. but i want this music. i want to listen to this music. because your words sounds like this melodies one sings before leaving their love, and i'm scared. maybe i'm trying to break your heart and mine before you do? but you never said you'd leave me. you only wanted me to not listen to songs. but i'm scared, scared. there are things running in my head, things that won't quieten down. things you didn't tell me. things i told you. i am suddenly feeling like you're leaving me and that scares me scares me. scares me more and more. but you're only trying to hold me on. if i told you it's as if you're singing those sad songs to me, you'd say i'm listening to too many sad songs. will you listen to the sad songs with me, please?"

5. hippocampus

"why is it so hard to forget? my brain must be made of seahorses. searhorses tend to store memories in the deepest layers of the ocean, and every time you cross the ocean, they sense you, and they get your memory. they're cute, but they're annoying. why do they have to remember the number of leaves on the tree that we sat under? (you had said, "i want to count the stars with you right now, but it's not night. so let's count the number of leaves on this tree. forget the stars now.") they remember the season of spring and fall, why do they tell me about the day we walked up to random people and told them to listen to my playlist? (you had told me, "people will forget what you gave, but will never forget the gift of music you gave them.") i want to forget all of you. not because you're no more here, because i'm no more here. seahorses aren't our favorite animals, but the ocean is. and like you loved me for my eyes, we would love the seahorses for the ocean. but I want them to stop. i want them to stop reminding me. remember when we got off into a car and it was raining, and you wouldn't let me drench? (you had said, "the rain will melt you and you'll forget me. so don't. please.") you were scared of being forgotten. you weren't that brave even though you were in love. nor am i. nor am i. that's why i can't forget. i can't forget. but i'm a fool. so i want to forget."

6. in love, in pain

"did you see the sky tonight? (but what if you break my heart?) it's brighter than the evening, which is strange, because evenings have the most goodbyes and goodbyes burn brighter. (my biggest problem is, i'd still love you.) i saw the breeze drift away through your eyelashes - has anyone told you that? (i'd dig in and love you.) it was a star that flickered far away – if think – it was talking to my poetess. (i'll be angry with myself but i'd still do it.) she bleeds on paper, she doesn't. (i'd love with a broken heart and there is nothing more painful.) she can't. (no there's something more painful - loving with a broken heart the person who broke it.) i can't. (i only wanted love; please don't make it hurt so much.)"

7. confession poetry

i cannot believe
that i am actually indulging in direct confession poetry that
my teacher taught me in class
but here i am
here's to all of you – you who?
read below.

remember when you
were young – like first grade young
and those early days –
you did so well, scored so good
and your parents were so proud to have you.
you became the teacher's favourite
the star of the class
a step ahead than many others in class.
obedient, brilliant, intelligent.
till date, you perhaps have no idea how you did it
that spotlight was your spot
the darkness beyond that spotlight – scary,
which you did not know back then.
years pass – a few
and dramatically things go wrong
you never scored those scores

for yourself – and you don't know how it happened.
you thought those marks are for yourself.
you thought those marks were yours –
and suddenly
it is as if a ghost had conjured them all this while.
you still cannot understand how you did that.
if you could do it all these years, why are you miserably
failing?
why cannot you be that perfect scorer?
and in no time you open your eyes after having shut them in
fear
you are standing in the darkness not the spotlight
you are not sure if you really had wanted that spotlight in the
first place
but now you are in a darkness
which you don't want now,

an increased tension along these years slowly escalating,
now stationary in your limbs – a heavy fear upon your head
your parents and teachers wonder what's gone wrong with you
and blame all those things that you fling yourself to
to stay out of this fear.
maybe you tried telling them – maybe you did not
"exam fears" is an understatement and the other kids will
never know what this feels like.

8. the colours are just not colourful enough and i want to scream that to their faces but they won't listen.

i've set up candles to blow, or rather,

time is a rolling moss stone unstopped and rolling

(life the moss, space the moisture.)

candles have been set to be blown

but they said they can't get me a red candle.

red, for i was 8 years old when i wanted to be in a beautiful body and not mine. (i didn't want my face either.)

they said they won't get me a green candle

green, for i was 13 years old when i wanted best friends, and i wanted boys to fall in love with me.

nor would they get me a pink candle

pink, for when i was 16 years old i fell for a boy. but i was a good girl that everybody wanted, and if they knew i was in love, they won't want me anymore.

i couldn't get a blue candle

blue, for i was 19 years old when i knew what drowning felt like.

they say they've placed 20 candles each in a colour.
(the air is too light and i'm drowning, the fire on the candles
too bright and i'm falling deeper.)
but all i can see are black and white, glitched, candles
and they say i need to look with more optimism.

9. grey earphones

"you sound like the grey earphones i've plugged in now. it is an impulsive decision, you know, to live. or is it? death isn't an impulsive decision – let me make it clear. they're well-crafted decisions that we control, we don't, we can control, we can't, we will control, we won't. but they're not decisions. they're choices, maybe that's why they call them impulsive. but i'm sure no one told you that living is impulsive too. they didn't lie my dear, life is just something that's too familiar. something so familiar cannot be impulsive is it. oh, you remind me of the grey earphones i'm wearing. the sky greyened this evening with messages i wanted to scream at your face – look at me talking as if i'd forgotten to tell you. i did not forget, but i didn't remember either. people with social anxiety practice "here" for hours honey,so that they say it properly. how did you expect me to say "help" within a lifetime?"

10. a monologue between me and me

close your eyes looking at the sky

you want to think about your life?

remember the time that they told you that you were fat and laughed

and for the rest of your life you measured your worth based on how the fat in your body was aligned?

close your eyes.

remember only these.

remember only the times you reminded yourself of not being worthy enough?

pretty much your entire life so far.

remember when there was a loud noise in your house and for the rest of your life loud noises are your ear's least favorite noises yet the noises they search to paralyze you?

remember when someone loved you and stopped all of a sudden and never told you why and for the rest of your life you think that at slightest expression of you people will walk away?

remember.

close your eyes.

you can only remember something you that you forgot

- tears reek out of my lashes -

tell me, what colour are they?
because memories have to be colourful.
so what stain have these tears made on my face?
none, none.
my brain knows for sure that it can see colours
but the colours get lost by the time they travel to my tongue.
there is only one colour my brain remembers -
they say that as time goes,
people become feelings
and feelings become people
the brain remembers things as it pleases
it remembers memory as colours
and colours as memory.
there is only one colour my brain remembers -
it's perhaps best called "sadness".

11. hurts like heaven

how can something hurt like heaven?

you uncover wounds with flowers, and crush it under the smell of the sky. you slap your hands across the grass, and lie that it doesn't hurt. it hurts, but you're too nice to even tell yourself that it hurts. by now, the flowers have been made into potions. drink it. it tastes of everything you almost had, but then you realize there's also a tint of things you never tasted. how would it feel to feel not in pain? this numbness, this is a bliss, the clouds would say. the skies would sing psalms of wounds you didn't deserve.

how can something hurt like heaven?
by making you believe that not feeling pain is heaven.

how can something hurt like heaven?
by making heaven a house and hell a home.

how can something hurt like heaven?
lies. all pain hurts like heaven and hell. they're liars. all pain inside bolts like heaven and hell.

how can something hurt like heaven?

12. puzzles

we love puzzles.
and that's why you speak in morse
and i in poetry.
keeping ourselves better off mysterious
we laugh with pride with our skills
yet you and i both
we die a little
every time someone doesn't care to unfurl us.
but there has always been something
both of us have never been able to code or poetize
though we are too good at hearing or seeing it.
we look at each other longingly
- we both know
but the world is not us.
we are our world but the world is not us.
and till the end it will be me and me or you and you or between us
because you'll never be able to code and i'll never be able to poetrize "help".

13. hiding in my room

the lights i decorate dangle from the ceiling
oblivious of the darkness i am trying to hide using them.
i rise my head as someone enters,
and my heart skids a beat while my lips curve a smile.
don't look beyond the smile, i pray. don't look into the eyes.
the room is bright like sunshine, like moonlight,
like starry decorations, pleasant for the eyes.
my eyes - they play along the light.
i am aware of the dusky twilight escaping my wrists
that i cut with the pieces of who i am not.
the lips smile, the lights still oblivious.
the stench of my heaviness escape when i'm alone,
but i do not want to switch off the lights.
i'm scared.
my scars glow in darkness, and
i don't want anyone to enter the room now even when i know
no one will.
no.
the lights are oblivious and that's why i keep them on.
i'm oblivious of how long i can sit underneath
the oblivious light, and the light thus stays on, stays oblivious,
for me.

14. i have a list of people that i don't want to come to my funeral

i have a list of people
that i don't want to come
to my funeral

i live in two different moments
or i wish i actually did.

my brain has only two thought trains that i can see:
(i don't know how many are hidden)
the what ifs and the could'ves

trust me i can try to give optimism over them but they aren't
my brain is a sick place
my funeral is where i live
a few things dead a few things alive
i take care of the arrangements here
i even have things too dead to die (maybe i'll tell you about
them some day)
some deaths murders
most murders suicides

(as i'd label the cases to avoid complications)
the too-dead-to-die, the alive, the dead require trigger
warnings
they're all quite sensitive
i don't have the required energy
to shield them all
so let me put up a trigger warning caution
the list of people
that i don't want in my
funerals.

15. incognito

i've been observing and catching feelings from around me
hoping to imprint and imitate them
because mine no longer seem to work.
(feelings are my cloths)

they're incognito -
their cover is numbness
(numbness is a closet i brought during a silent night and ever
since it has not been something that obeys me)

they refuse to step out of the closet and
i've been sitting naked for days
for days
leaning against the closed doors

it's not my fault
that my options
are a multiple-choice system
where all buttons have gone haywire
and they're all blinking

was it really a choice though
(to have them?) my wrists ache from banging on the door; but

how?
i thought i couldn't feel anything
(if the ghost knew i knew it was looking, it hid)
maybe if i stopped feeling, i would feel

my fingers feel soft when they go numb
my fingers are soft when they go numb.

it is strange that
their brittleness has such strength
and
their fragility
is their shield
(i don't know for what. they never tell me)

maybe if i touch stars they'd be soft too?

my fingers and the stars
they both have fought darkness
and have
held dreams on their shoulders

i'd even rubbed my fingers against the closet
hoping to tickle
my feelings out

but i am glad i stopped

trying

even when i wanted them to step out
i know
that they would get behind me
to hide from what i don't know
but will end up pushing me
into the closet

and i would scream

but my fingers will remain soft from the numbness
(numbness is like a tinge of fairydust that my fingers carry
anywhere
maybe numbness is soft afterall
but neither brittle nor weak.)

16. reasons to not love me

i. my hands will shake when i miss you. when i miss you, i make it feel like you are dead, by crying and feeling my insides clawing against my skins. i'll miss you more than you should be missed.

ii. i will expect you to spend time with me even in the busiest of times. i will expect you to explain. when you don't, i sit there wishing you would explain.

iii. i don't even know why i'm writing this poetry.

iv. i don't know if what i write are poetry.

v. i tell random things when i'm afraid to tell you that i love you.

vi. i will suffocatingly love you that i'd be wishing i could hate you.

vii. i'll make you immortal by putting pieces of you in my words.

viii. if i'm angry with you, i will expect you to come to me but i'll run to you before you even know i'm angry with you.

so please don't fall in love with me.

because from the above points, it is hence proved that i'm a coward in love.

17. if you never met the right love, remember me.

we were too young, we should've chosen the wrong choice if this was wrong but we gave up. so if you never met the right love, i want you to remember me.

i thought you told me that you loved me but i don't know. i did not look into your eyes when told me that you loved me, because i thought i turned paranoid of wanting love. if you never met the right love, i want you to remember me.

i never made anything simple for anyone, and your hands were too tired to hold me whilst you were falling down. so you closed your eyes and let me go. but if you never met the right love, i want you to remember me.

i didn't feel right in your guts, and i never made you feel right. and when you came forward to make it right, i was too desperate, and you weren't sure if you could handle a hanging cliff. so you took a walk. when you are on your way back and never met the right love, i want you to remember me.

i've been a little too tired to move from where i'd been left but i'd been climbing upwards slowly. i'm a little too lost from where i was left behind so i've been taking careful steps against the insanity.

so if you never met the right love, i want you to remember me.

18. once you fall in love with things you can't have, you don't fall out of love of it.

"i know you're going to stop talking to me after tonight, but remember the first time i tried to take an earphone off your ear and you pushed me away? you said you don't share music with strangers. the next time i tried, you showed me what song you were listening to, but you didn't allow me to listen to it with you, and i didn't know what song it was either. then later i'd lay on your chest listening to your heart hoping i'd get a glimpse of the music you listen to. when you listen to music every night, i'd sit in front of you, quietly watching you. you would look at me too, but i'd know that it'd be your music that unfurls in front of your eyes. did you see me when you looked at me? how did i look to your eyes then? last night, i tried taking your earphone and listen, but you pushed me away. you said you don't share music with a lover. i don't want you to take me back, but can you let me in this night, and let me plug in your earphone with you? i really want to listen to your song."

19. you loved crushing dahlias

"stop. just... STOP. stop moving away from me stop pushing me away! what is possibly the darkest thing you could've done? murder someone? how is it dark? i've been right here in front of your eyes, and every time you move away, i've been blaming it on me and killing myself. i've been rearranging the dahlias on the bouquet - my best friend told me there are no dahlia bouquets but you said you loved crushing them so i bought them for you as a bouquet and they look at my face every day asking me if i love you so much that i'd let you crush them, the flowers i tenderly collected. i've been letting you kill me, why not a few flowers? they lie there on my table looking at my face asking if they'd ever go home. how long has it been since i've been home? i've been living inside my body but have i been there really? tell me, why are you moving away? how much darkness do you think you have? is it any darker than me killing myself? is it harder than me choosing you every time over me? i never even ask you to choose me. but just... love me and touch me like those dahlias you've touched. and kill me. because if i keep going, i'd only kill me, stuff myself inside myself and kill myself more, because i don't really die, you know. i don't die. but if you could, kill me. kill me before you move away once again because you're... no, you're not a dark person for who you are, but you're a dark person for stamping on me every day and still making me be in love with you so much. why am i in love with you so much? is it even love? i don't know what love is now. i don't know. i really don't. i really don't know."

20. fading rain

this fading rain brings me back to reality, to you.

i grow tired of love, darling. i'm tired of the frantic heartbeat that accompanies it. i'm tired of the claustrophobia of losing someone. i'm tired of the evanescencing warmth. but i know that is about how i take in love. i either obsess or hate. i'd go for all distances for just one smile someone gives. my hands, they're scorched of those bonds that i lit up and those that were lit, of those burning bonds that i refused to let go.

i know you have a self to take care of, but you did ask me of the core of my raging stars. every time i meet your eyes, i'm scared. i want to give this a try, but i conflict myself by imagining you letting me go, that all the ropes i threw you up to pull myself out will burn away and i shall fall again into the pit whose end is fading.

charcoalic coldness, rusted breezes, dazed night skies, the moon dripping with tears, fading nebulas, falling crusts, screaming skies, shuddering cliffs and silent voids.

this is also me. i am learning to love this part of me. my crests are shaking, my pens unable to trace poetries.

will you stay till i grow back after the rain? maybe i'm greedy, but can you help me hold my pieces together and drench alongside in this rain?

21. perfume bottle

i see the purple liquid inside the perfume bottle, and nothing entices me about it. i'm making it a part of my poetry even as it just sits there lonely and quiet, and i'm not sure why. i had decided i wouldn't keep writing about all things lonely and quiet; i had decided i wouldn't keep being homes of all broken things.

i'm not even sure if this perfume really is all things lonely and quiet, and of broken pieces, but i imagine the smell of the perfume to distract myself. i wouldn't walk to it and smell it. i don't want to make it enticing to my senses and get drunk in it.

because i quite know i'd remember your scent if i take it. i don't want you to be my muse but i keep making it happen. i let your fragrance break my insides and keep you at the circumference of my viewpoint.

well i envy you. even in this darkness where even the silhouettes aren't clear, you become the purple liquid of the glass bottle sitting on the shelf. maybe in the morning, the liquid wouldn't look purple. but i'm afraid the stench of it would cripple me into all things rotten in my head.

i can hear the glass bottle emit a silence that your memories do. an emptiness. it's as if you are a part of my veins, and a part of me settles back comfortably at that. you could destroy

me and let me drown, but i'd still see what you are made of, even if it kills me. you and your memories make me get scared of my own shadows, but i'd sit like that perfume bottle finally, lonely and quiet, assuming it is, but somehow enticing, that i'd etch your memory lanes as a ghost. and maybe somehow, someone else would dive in to push away the murk of you i let in my fragrance.
maybe i'd find love.

22. fur dolls.

"come inside here - i know it's not the fog on the window that makes you look you like that. i know the firewood inside is dimming too - but you remember the times you hugged me tight pretending you were fine? where are the blazes underneath the coal of your eyes? where are the silences inside your ear? where is the frost underneath your skin? where are your shadows? come here, you don't have to hide them from me. you don't have to hide yourselves from them. darling, i know all harsh words have rung inside your ears that you wished to listen to the dripping honey, and wondered if you had been over-expecting. i know you've been telling yourselves a lot of things, things you know you aren't supposed to tell yourself. come over here, there are parts of you that you love, there are parts you hate. there are parts you don't know what to do with. there are parts that haven't been loved enough. there are parts of you i know you wish you could kill. the parts of you that you are trying hard to love, trying hard to hate. darling, when i say i love you, i love all of it. whether you like it or not. i know they're all parts of you. why wouldn't i love your little pieces, and help you with what you need? please, let me love you in places you haven't been loved, have been loved, have been hated, have been ruined, have been destroyed, have been built, have been created. please let me have you."

23. withered leaves

your presence wasn't much of a wind,

yet there is a string of your presence subtly deep around.

there were the whispering strokes of the midnight silences

floating warmly in the air,

no wonder i feel a little heat surge

in the coldness around me.

there were the brushes your memories

told me in my ears,

no wonder i feel my wilted edges a little blushed.

there were your touches that embraced my existence,

no wonder i feel a hovering shadow in this empty darkness.

the midnight continues in a dawn of veiled evanesces

of who i am, but then, i feel a mustling aura

holding me at the edge of the clashing cliffs.

well of course darling.

withered leaves seldom fall against the breeze.

24. you and breeze

the leaves chingled with each other in the morning breeze,
the sunrays careful enough
to not fall between them and disturb them.
quietly,
the breeze outside the sunrays borrows the warmth,
scurries to rub slightly against those sleepy leaves.
it was a bliss to watch them, darling.
remember the evening walks we used to go
and the morning walks we plan to go?
i bet our hands will be those leaves.
but I doubt if my fingers would want
to be broken up from that slumber.
did the leaf want to be rubbed?
i don't know.
yet the breeze *will* play between our hands
won't they?
because your fingers are what
that shushes the breeze
not to wake mine but also
what the breeze want to stay into.
and i am not getting into this
magnetic confusion between you and the breeze.
because i know that your poetries are homes

to breezes and

the breezes cannot stay away from you.

and i'd make through adoring

the lively cuddles between you and the breeze disguised as

tiffs,

leaning back to dot all the magic around me.

25. getting lost

you said i can't get lost in familiar places but i do get lost in poetry.

you said i can't get lost in places where there is light but i do get lost in darkness.

you said i can't get lost in unobscure places, but i do get lost in your eyes.

you said i can't get lost inside my house when my eyes are open, but i do get lost inside my body.

you said i can't get lost in places i'd never go, but i do get lost in the stench of your fragrance.

you said i can't get lost in things i haven't forgotten, but i do get lost in empty sheets.

you said i can't get lost, i can't get lost, but i do.

it is not familiar places where you can't get lost –

it is in places where you don't want to find yourself that you get lost,

in places you don't have to ache to be lost that you cannot be found.

and you say, "lost" as if one can be found back, found back.

To All Things I Love

to all things i love and yet i don't do.

i don't know where to start, and in that space that i walk with hesitance, blankness, helplessness, loss and humility, is where i start.

not many things make the soul. i think some strings of existence were severed – have you heard of a social media theory on soulmates? the stranger suggested that soulmates are people whose atoms were close by each other when the universe was created. and i think that is true with what speaks to the soul. i think we're all connected by trails of nerves that we don't see and understand, and that our minds are all connected in a fast-maze of sparks travelling and light year, and that is why every thought is already thought by someone, and the existence of a thought is an indication of someone else having it (fascinating and horrifying, and that reminds me of how i never think so of love for me.)

i think all things i love speak to me – skies, clouds, sun, moon, stars, trees, breeze, rain, lightning, writing and all of that – and yet i don't do them. funny – we were put on this earth, or perhaps choose to go on, for all these things, and yet, i ignore doing them. i am not sure when that habit began, but it did, and i kept going with it. the amount of time i spent doing anything i love kept going down. and every time it would feel like it is going to cease, something happens, and i keep going with it.

i assumed that what you want to do, what you love to do, will always be there, and that is only partly correct. it never occurred to me that you may not have energy to do things you love, and love, isn't default, isn't noble, doesn't exist in void, but takes up space and thus ultimately a burden. not as a evaluative feature but in a purely numerical value.

i don't think i am as divine as all that i love. i feel like i am chosen, even though it may feel like a poetic exaggeration of something mundane that sounds spectacular because of cosmic insignificance and size. (here i am – having an external dialogue and wanting to put in an excuse to defend my feeling.) anyways. what i am trying to say is lost again in reasons how i slowly lost it all. a severe urge to keep running, keep running, from me. when did running from me become more important than embracing what i love? with sheer pride, it makes me think that what i love is more of me, just as what i am running from is.

and so it goes – embracing me would be the antidote to hating me, but the energy to do is consumed by hating me, and/or in hating me. coming so far in this writing. some times (many times) the part that wants to run away and does run away wins, and it's all that i remember. escaping. from what i don't remember anymore. maybe sitting with this grief will get me back to love, because, that is what i heard grief is – love persevering. perhaps, if i sit long enough with the grief, i will discover it has a different name, and a body to be hugged. and a body to be embraced. perhaps, if i pause and ask myself, "do you want me to sit in the darkness? we don't have to make everything into art", then i will slowly thread myself to love, thread myself through grief, thread myself to me.

to all the things i love and yet i don't do – it won't stay that way.

3 Poems That I Rewrote To My Fullest Glory

there is a road that goes down into a tunnel, traversing it's tar and cement and paste – to think that the roads stay together because of those who travel on it or because of those who built it is stupid, because, they stay together because of the people who decided roads should exist, that paths should exist, that the people who decided roads should exist, that travelling must be passed down, that is it inevitable, because we're all but travelers, because journeys are not determined by those who walk but by existence, because power have us but we all of us however don't have power – and will i ever know if the road stopped for the tunnel to take over, or if the tunnel took over the road? but why do things exist in my head to think, why do i think? thinking. thinking. that is what it is. that is what exists. not the road, not the tunnel, not the paste, not the people. thinking. or, thoughts? the verb and the noun are a *continuum*.

leaves fall of trees, but will i ever know if the tree is sad, because leaves fall, and autumn makes it lonely? leaves stay, but will i ever know if the tree is heavy, because leaves stay, and spring makes it heavy? how lonely is loneliness? how much does heaviness weigh? do trees talk in the language of fall to hustle their heaviness out into the air, and that's why, the leaves falls? do trees talk in the language of spring to lyricize their loneliness, and that's why, the leaves remain? what language of the trees do the trees actually speak? loneliness or heaviness? do we really listen to the breeze? the language. *the language in the breeze.*

i speak in silence, i scream in silence. chaos speaks a *tongue* that is in *continuum* with silence, that is all that i know. but chaos' words haven't brushed my ear and sent a chill down my spine, neither has a lover's lips. but every time i sit in class, amongst other people, i realize it's the other way around. the fibers of my existence are caught between the north and south poles of this confusion, and when i'm asked what i want to be, i want to tell them that i want to be two people, that i should've been two people all along, that people should be given the chance to be two people, that nature functions wrong and stuffs only one person inside one person. but i do not say anything – i smile, and that's my chaotic silence. or my silence chaos? *the verb and noun are a continuum in the breeze's language, but what do my feelings speak?*

and i balter abditorily in existence, because all things i encompass are immortal, become immortal, and that is how existence spells out itself through the tips of our fingers.

i have a conspiracy theory that if poets had ruled the world, they would have called the universe to be cordiformed, but they didn't, and also, that's why they didn't rule the world. i have a conspiracy theory that the universe is sad, and that is why poets are made. i have a conspiracy theory that this sadness as been pressed down for ages, and that is why poetries are diamonds. i have a conspiracy theory that the universe has clinomania, and that is why poetries are lullabies. i have a conspiracy theory that the noise inside my head is the noise of metal screeching, and that is why i find it hard to stay in my body. i have a conspiracy theory that the universe will never stop being sad for another thousand years, and that is why art is immortal. i have a conspiracy theory that the universe searches for rainbows to paint itself, and that is why it rains. i have a conspiracy theory that we all know deep down that we'll never escape the universe nor can we make it happy, and that's why we look at colours, that's why everything is aesthetic. i have a conspiracy theory that the tears blinded the universe's eyes while creating, and that is why some of us keep searching something that we don't know what. i have a conspiracy theory that we all search outside of us where we came from, and that is why we love the stars. i have a conspiracy theory that we're all trying to heal the universe and that is why love exists. i have a conspiracy theory that if we look as far as our eyes can wander in the night sky we'll see the universe looking back at us, and that is why we don't look up at the sky anymore. i have a conspiracy theory that we don't look into ourselves, into the universe, and that is why the universe keeps making a propaganda of its sadness – it really needs to stop sending in more broken people.

i have a conspiracy theory that if poets had ruled the world, they would have called the universe to be cordiformed, but they didn't, that's why they didn't rule the world, and instead, they're sad, and they yearn, and their sadness becomes poetry; but the poets never do, they never are poetry, because if they are, they would have written about them.

and the universe lets out another heavy sigh – it's time for me to write.

how long has it been since i've threaded sadness together? nobody asks me for a manual to make me sad, because they can do it themselves, and they never know they make me sad, so they poke me with a stick to see if i'm sad enough, sad enough.

but before i go to sleep, i write down three ways to make me sad, and i know no one wants to read it – but i write down five ways to make me sad.

1. ask me about the things i love, and i will say that it's the sky. and so i will remember how i've not been loving it enough. guilt haunts me, and i realize that here is only fear everywhere. everywhere. *i don't love less because i'm not capable of love, i love less because i don't want to be capable of love.*

2. ask me the places i wish i never went to, the places i wish to forget so that i start talking about my body. i will think about how i take too much space and i am too much weight and how i don't feel like existing but puking when i'm at parties and how i'm so humble that i starve myself to save the food that's always enough for everyone. *i can never stop wanting to be look different, not because no one loves the way i look but because there's no room here for love and i don't want to stop hugging the hate, because love makes me think i'm enough but i'm not, i'm not.*

3. give me a little attention and i'll give you all of my heart, so that when you say you don't love me, which you will, i can cry about how you promised you'd love me and you can tell me that you never promised you will, and that i'm being demandy that my heart is never worthy enough to be taken care like yours or someone else who is not me. *i don't crave attention because i don't get it, but because*

it makes me feel comfortable, for love is too big and too nice for me to be a deserving person.

i'm pretty good at breaking what exists as whole, keep it together and tell everyone that it's indeed an whole and that i'm in love with all things broken, but perhaps that is why i break my heart, that is why i write down ways to break my heart, so that i can finally love it. I love sad people and that perhaps is why i'm looking for ways to be sad, to wear sad, and maybe, people will love me when i'm sad. so here's a fourth way to break my heart:

4. i am filled with hope easily. what fills my barren lungs is not my own oxygen supply. so, you need to leave me and walk away. when you go, you take your air with you, and i'm filled with your air, your hope, and every time i breath, i can't scrub it off. *i don't gasp for air because i can't breathe, i gasp because i have too much air that is not mine.*

Tacenda

It would make sense only to an artist that the sky and the ground are not crude, philosophical, unidentical reflections but extensions with the same adjectives of each other, their meanings seemingly empty but full, seemingly full but empty, a balance that will collapse if it doesn't exist without this intricacy. In this most unpoetic way, it is an exhaustive battle of boundaries of quip that the bundles of nerves in our brain cans stretch itself to.

The sky and the ground are stuck separately with endless proofs of infinity – the most brilliant and the most foolish that the Universe has done is to make infinity a relative concept.

As an artist, it is inescapable of me to not have darkness in my head. While it is only human to have so, it is an artist's eternal question to wonder whether they're consuming and coating themselves with this darkness or if they're running away from it in lightning speed. But to be more accurate, this confusion doesn't represent the artist's run, but their *beginning* – the beginning of the time in their life that they decide to/are forced with being an artist. What represents their journey then? Running? Caged? Do they ever know? Well, I know that *I* don't know. The Universe made this a tacenda for its own reasons.

I am one of those people – I hope and believe I can never be truly alone – who are caught in an endless run of feeling the pain yet telling themselves they're exaggerating. And I am stuck – I do not reside – inside a clock. The glass in front of me – what lies ahead of the glass is not a point of discussion – is cracked but doesn't break and fall off. It is ruptured so well together that I wonder if it is the rupture that holds the glass together. Little grains of glass however, fall over me all the time. I wonder if I'm exaggerating it – even when I know pain is relative, and pain is valid, that relativity and valid can and does exist in the midst of Venn Circles of Pain and Relativity, nothing can convince me to believe that I'm not exaggerating. Pain and suffering are very intricate matters – every pain is valid, but pain, is relative, and that makes pain non-existent for those who cannot relate with it, or does it?

Sadness is over me, inscribed into the skin that I wear, like an allegation, like fairies and goblins, like madness, that would ruin my life if I say out loud, that when I say out loud I would perhaps die, that I'd remain a madperson and be celebrated by people posthumously. But I cannot die. So, I silence myself. To write about silence in silence, to write about pain in pain, is romanticized by poets, but it isn't inspiring in real. It is silence, it is pain.

I do want to write about my pain (how can you write about happiness if you cannot write about pain?) but this is the time of that my pen refuses to move to script my pain, because I have no sadness, because I have no pain. At this point of life, it is hard for me to recall any part of me or my life and write about it, or to write about sadness, because you can write only what you own, only what you believe you own, only what you want to own. Am I so hopeless that I don't fall under any of these? It's tacenda. The only fairytale I have, that I dare and ache to share is that my writing is now under a demonic spell that I can only break with a true love's kiss but I'm a coward. There is no hero here. Is there love? Perhaps. But there is no hero here, and it is called a fairytale only because it has a demon in it. To be a writer, or more aptly, to be someone who has publicly announced herself as a writer – how would you feel if you woke up one day and realized that you have forgotten how it is to live? Does it make sense? No. That is how my pain is when I want to script it. But is it sad? Yes. That is undeniably what I have.

Two roads diverged in front of me and I took the one less travelled – that is perhaps what I script. Because silence hovers around me – or is it me – and tells me there is no pain, tells the world there is no pain. So what is is about my life that I shall script? My weakness that stops me from breaking the glass of the clock and stepping out of it? My sadness that is my secret affair? I seem to be capable of scripting only what that is not mundane – and writing down my struggles seem so, even though in my head they don't. So I numb me, I silence me, and the water has slowly flooded through every memory, every event, and now, I have a photo album with numerous pages I lost, some that I tore and the rest that is now soaked. It's tacenda.

To be haunted by my own home, to wonder who the monsters in my head are – to resist, resist and to write. To douse all the burnt matches and use that graphite to sketch a map on the ground hoping I remember well the constellations I see every night. To be stubborn to not use mundane psychological terms to label and dissect and lay out the monsters in my head in an essay I've written for others to read and instead sculpt the pain in a hauntingly beautiful yet insidiously creepy way. To be. To write. To be. To write.

And amidst all that, I spawn cosmic stardust I steal with all the darkness in my head – and in this Universe, I'm a memory.

• 48 •

"a Child Looking Out My Window"

""… I'm forever a child looking out my window at the night sky, Thinking one day I'll touch the world with bare hands, Even if it burns." – Tracy K. Smith, from "Don't You Wonder, Sometimes?", Life on Mars"

After all that is said and done, it is not history that remembers but humanity that remembers it and passes it down. And ages later, we look back at one piece of art, and in one eye of it, we see something glisten because memories we've carried down in our head ache to find a place where they're reflected, and we find new meanings. That is how we remember.

We scream around in our social media pages, 'This is not what we signed up for when we screamed "Happy New Year"!' Three months into 2020, and we are letting someone else fight a battle as if it's their own, and we sit nicely cuddled and warmed up in our cloaks of privilege.

The novel Corona Virus, or the SARS-CoV-2, dawned out and still remains as more than just a health pandemic – there is a certain worry that arises inside me, or fear, if I have to strengthen my case, when I wonder if we will ever heal from what this pandemic has caused us, from what we've caused ourselves. This pandemic has been a time of being unhygienic with our information processing, selectively consuming data down every bite and sip, data that reinforces what out brain already believes, beliefs of collective insecurity.

And then when days start, the fibers of my heart keep getting stretched beyond how much I think it cans stretch – the world is not anything close to a safe space, and as annoyingly optimistic person, I refuse to be "positive" about "progress". So what has changed for me amidst this? Hope.

George Floyd couldn't breathe, countless names are still names and every protestor for every cause is just reckless, young and wild who just vibe with the crowd, refugees are quite free enough to catch on any pandemic and die, Uighur Muslims have no God to run to and so many other religions decide who is worthy of reaching God, Siberia didn't rig bombs but election like many other countries (and perhaps bombs too, and violence, but the protestors were asking for it anyways), pictures of children from Yemen surfaced up our feed but food didn't surface up theirs, children were to be hugged and kissed a goodnight but instead they went missing because they were Mexican immigrants, Philippines took it up as its norm to decide value if human relationships like many other countries, Palestine, Kashmir, Syria, Afghanistan among others ache about how long they'll be invisible, the Environmental Impact Assessment became an inconvenience, punishing those who mistreated people with disabilities was a threat to business, Men's Rights Activists would keep quiet on a father-son duo murdered by police, but, we're all just overreacting.

It was never about 2020. Years are counted on a homosapien's maturity, and so, 2020 is not a predetermined year. Nothing much is permanently predetermined. It's about how each of us humans chooses to shroud ourselves.

So what has changed for me amidst this? Hope. I've gone into countless mental health breaks even in a single day, and I still cannot ignore the world. It's as if we were all born tired and that is perhaps why our revolution is fought with even more reverence and sincerity, like every breath is our last, like we will not go down without a fight. Revolution is here, right here, in front of all our eyes, and we're already into it. The battle is happening, and each of us is already a part of it, and will always be.

The beautiful thing, however, is that we have in our hands countless ways to fight. Art is political, art is resistance, and we're all artists of our own kind, because there is no one singular art, and art is meant to be felt not perfect, and each of us are felt and loved and have love in us, and each of us are not our calendar years but ideas and action, and all cosmic uniqueness and similarity that the Universe conspired to be, masterpieces. Revolution and poetry may not seem to go well with each other, but there is no revolution without poets and no poetry without revolutionists. It is beautiful that each of us has our place on this Earth, of our own kind, and each of it is valid, nothing comparable or replaceable.

Artists put strokes of paint for all of us to see, and we forcefully crane the neck of those who refuse to turn and see. We're shining light in the eyes of those who refuse to open their eyes and observe. We mutter and stutter and talk and scream into the ears of those who shut it tight. And once art goes in, it kindles the art we have and the art we are, and to express art is unstoppable.

We're all in this mesh, and nothing is truer than that. Art has come alive, revolution has streaked everyone, poets are melancholic idiots, and each of that is helping each of us in different ways. It is insufferable to wait, and none of us are immortal. But that is what we changed amidst this – something we've always quaintly done, an essence of being human. Ideas.

Ideas are not going to be food for empty plates or plasters for wounds or ventilators for life. But the world isn't going anywhere, and humans easily go hopeless and then get back up again – we're sunflowers, and according to the popular idea, the sunflowers face the sun when it's up and face each other when it is not. We can hate each other as much as we want, and maybe it's just survival instincts, but we'll stick with each other. As much as messy it is, we're all going to thread together. We're going to leave behind legacies of hope.

So what has changed for me amidst this? Hope. Perhaps we don't see it now, but humanity will remember our hope. Every little thing we do does count, and humanity will carry hope without knowing it, and it will grow, grow. And we'll love and heal.